HOCKEY HAIKU

Other Titles by These Authors

My Big Fat Hockey Haiku

Derian Hatcher: A Goon's Goon

*What to Expect When You're Expecting
A Hockey Haiku*

The Hockey Haiku of Madison County

A Million Little Hockey Haikus

The Lion, The Witch, and the Hockey Haiku

The Fellowship of the Hockey Haiku

So You Want to Be a Hockey Haikuist

*Modernist Hockey Haiku and the
Vegetarian Mind*

*Mid-Evil or Medieval? A History of the
Center Line*

The Satanic Hockey Haiku

A Buyer's Guide to Rare Hockey Haiku

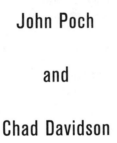

John Poch

and

Chad Davidson

HOCKEY HAIKU

The

Essential

Collection

THOMAS DUNNE BOOKS / ST. MARTIN'S GRIFFIN ✦ NEW YORK

THOMAS DUNNE BOOKS.

An imprint of St. Martin's Press.

HOCKEY HAIKU. Copyright © 2006 by John Poch and Chad David-son. All rights reserved. Printed in the United States of America. No part of this book may be used or reproduced in any manner whatsoever without written permission except in the case of brief quotations embodied in critical articles or reviews. For informa-tion, address St. Martin's Press, 175 Fifth Avenue, New York, N.Y. 10010.

www.thomasdunnebooks.com

www.stmartins.com

Book design by Susan Walsh

Library of Congress Cataloging-in-Publication Data

Davidson, Chad, 1970–
    Hockey haiku / by Chad Davidson and John Poch.—1st ed.
        p. cm.
    EAN-13: 978-0-312-35607-1
    ISBN-10: 0-312-35607-2
        I. Poch, John, 1966–

PS3604.A946H63 2006
811'.6—dc22

                                        2006043876

First Edition: October 2006

10 9 8 7 6 5 4 3 2 1

For Mike Modano, if he'll have it

Contents

Acknowledgments

We'd like to thank the literary journals where some of these hockey haiku first appeared: *Backwards City Review*, *DIAGRAM*, *The North Dakota Hockey Haiku Weekly*, *Redivider*, *SleepingFish*, and *Smartish Pace*. We'd also like to thank The Institute of Hockey Haiku in Nova Scotia and the library staff there, especially Wanda Kjorjikoff and Philip Pabst, for access to and assistance with original manuscripts. We couldn't have completed our work without a grant from the Northern Michigan (Upper Peninsula) Hockey Haiku Council. Commemorative Lady Byngs to Austin Hummell and Chad Parmenter for being our go-to researchers in Japan and Russia, respectively. Vezinas to Drs. John Mayfield and Jerry "Tin Can" Shearer—the very essence of Hockey Haikudom both—for saving us when we began to flag. Also, we must recognize our wives, Gwen

Davidson and Meghan Poch—our own personal "Latvian netminders"—for their patience and encouragement toward the completion of this book. Sean Desmond, you are the smooth and solid ice beneath our skates. We condemn utterly and publicly the Winnipeg School.

A limited edition of twenty-five hockey haiku were printed as broadsides in celebration of Mike Modano's thirtieth birthday.

Introduction

While historians and enthusiasts alike argue hopelessly over the hockey haiku's official beginnings, its history remains shrouded in myth. Some talk generally of its inception during the decline of the Samurai class in Japan, suggesting that the ritualized aggression and disciplined servitude of the Samurai were displaced and ultimately projected onto the prehockey haiku form once hockey came to dominate the imaginations of the Pacific Rim nations.[1] Even though its lineage could be traced back to Japan, how hockey haiku

---

[1] Also of historical importance is the proliferation of modern photocopiers, which allowed for the production of multiple copies of hockey haiku with relative ease and at minimal cost. While the art of calligraphic hockey haiku was nearly lost, the lower classes suddenly had access to the form once reserved for royalty. This is otherwise known as the "hockey haiku diaspora."

found a toehold in North America still baffles scholars.[2] We do know with some certainty that by the time of the "Miracle on Manchester" (Los Angeles, 1982)[3] hockey haiku had gained its full ascendancy.

Regardless of such misty origins, hockey haiku has inarguably become a curious mix, at once as ubiquitous as a top-shelf cookie jar and as protean as the cookies within. Ask any goon on the street and he will inevitably spin yarns about his grandfather whittling pygmy hockey sticks out of Scandinavian birch while reclining in his rocking chair, dictating hockey haiku to grandmother, cooking her miso in the kitchen. Or reed cutting with Uncle Yamamoto, his bellowing voice suddenly malleable, more inviting as he recited the classic hockey haiku he'd learned in school.

Who doesn't have a similar story, a similar life lived

---

[2] Canadian scholar and former Blackhawk Gus "Hooly" Hoolihan's research of ten years (1967–77), in which he attempted the Schliemannesque task of finding the Ur-hockey haiku in Japan, resulted in a broken marriage, four bouts of dysentery, mediocre competency in Japanese, and little proof beyond this fragment found on a scrap of parchment inside an abandoned locker at a suitcase factory in Nagoya, later dated to 1891: "Shining black in net / Stick high [word illegible] over ice / Whales don't win. . . ." What is fundamentally a problem of translating a corrupt original was compounded by the fact that both the former Hartford Whalers and the Norwegian whaling industry fervently argued the fragment's authenticity.

[3] When the underdog Los Angeles Kings defeated the Edmonton Oilers (among them, Gretzky) in their first-round matchup.

within the transgenerational umbrage of hockey haiku?[4] And to be sure, everyone writes hockey haiku. We are drawn by the seemingly contradictory equipoise and brutality inherent in its form and content. As with its prototype, the raw prehockey haiku—where the impulse was spontaneous, the strokes of the artist far past scrutiny, part of muscle memory—so, too, the sport of hockey. Ask any Art Ross Trophy winner after a pretty goal. He'll say the goal was not as much the motivation as it was the end result of mindlessness.[5] Put together the solitary discipline of haiku and the automatic grace of the hockey player: what you have is a perfect balance of yin and yang. Indeed, the refinements to the prehockey haiku form that came with its marriage to hockey, in hindsight, seem inevitable.

We might say that each element of this systemic art form counterbalances or "checks" the other. While a certain hockey haiku might detail in stunningly brave

---

[4] If either editor of this anthology were to show you his high school annual, you would see that nearly every other dedication either includes a complete hockey haiku or individual lines from the pop hockey haikuists of the mid-eighties.

[5] Bobby Hull once described a breakaway and shot to the net as enlightening, the heavily padded goalie before him suddenly transforming into an image of the Buddha, potbellied and frozen as a statue, which he was forced to honor by going top-shelf.

strokes the artful stickwork of a Pavel Bure, yet another might paint in quiet reverie the brutality of the game's darker side: paybacks as grotesque as any Mafia hit.[6] It is the unique ability of each element of hockey haiku to morph into its other. In so doing the form does not merely test our very notions of objective truth, it shatters them like so much Plexiglas under the force of an Al MacInnis slap shot. Hockey haiku, thus, represents the perfect harmony of Apollonian and Dionysian tendencies: graceful brutality, ordered chaos, the blood that courses through our veins, and, if we are unfortunate, onto the ice.[7]

Many critics have bandied about notions of the modern hockey haiku's illegitimacy, its seeming disdain for the "rules" set forth by the prehockey haiku masters.[8] Though it needs no apology, we offer instead a "reading" of the manners and exigencies of hockey haiku. Former U.S. poet laureate Robert Hass, in his moving

---

[6] Vide most recently Canuck Todd Bertuzzi's mauling of the Avalanche's Steve Moore (2003–4 season).

[7] Bashō claimed that "a poet needs to discipline himself every day." The same could be said for a hockey player.

[8] Anthony Hecht: "As the Sibyl of Cumae said: It takes all kinds." Nevertheless, we renounce the Winnipeg School of Criticism, which has made numerous claims that all white space is equal. Roland Barthes's characterization of hockey haiku's "breach of meaning" in *The Empire of Signs* is much more astute in its postmodern appraisal.

translation of prehockey haiku,[9] does away with the syllabic order of 5-7-5.[10] Our readers will notice that the poets we have selected for this anthology reinstated the syllabics. Their adherence to the preestablished, if prosodically foreign, syllable count recovers a good deal of prehockey haiku history. It also mimics, in its studied rigor, the facts of the hockey game: three periods, with the midperiod being elongated by the short intermissions on either side. But there are other strengths to the syllabic reinstatement. Think if the game of hockey were as elastic as Hass deemed the syllable count. Wayne Gretzky, for example, could not stop the sixth game of the 1993 Conference Finals against the Toronto Maple Leafs simply because he "didn't feel inspired." Matsuo Bashō—arguably the greatest of the prehockey haiku masters—claimed that a good haiku writer writes perhaps ten haiku in a day and keeps only one. At the end of the week he takes those seven re-

---

[9] Vide also Victor Seblitz's Hockey Haiku for Dummies, particularly his introduction dedicated to the oral traditions of hockey haiku still flourishing in the former Baltic states.

[10] The first official name for the Mullet, otherwise known as the Kentucky Waterfall, was "Hockey Hair." Jaromir Jagr, one of the most famous players to sport this do, knew he had fallen short of what could have vaulted him into Hockey Hair history when a fellow Czech, Robert Lang, arranged for his stylist to cut his hair in 5-7-5–inch proportions from front to back. Lang looked like a freak, but statistics show the haircut improved his game.

maining and keeps only one. At the end of the month he keeps one of the four. At the end of the year he keeps one of the twelve, and so on ad nauseam. Fine and well. But in hockey, there is no scrapping a game, no easy erasure.

Other critics[11] harp on the absence of subtle, seasonal references (*kigo* in Japanese). As we know, prehockey haiku masters were gifted in their ability to portray the time of year through focused and brief imagery: snow in the stirrups of a tethered horse; a spider gloating in the springtime sunbeams. For the masters of hockey haiku, the difficulty "snowballs." No matter what the season outside the arena, it is *always* winter inside. A blazing Phoenix afternoon suddenly becomes the frozen pond of an Edmonton suburb. Likewise, the subzero, near-Dantean cold of eastern Minneapolis, at least for a few hours, becomes bearable again, a predictable climate, the seats full of sloughed-off puffycoats, mittens, and scarves.[12]

---

[11] Many of them under the spell of their Winnipeg School pre-post-postmodern thinking, actually prefer roller blades to ice skates. This is akin to preferring Billy Idol over Billy Squier. They fail to recognize that Pound's dictum "make it new" did not dismiss the Chinese written character but bowed to it.

[12] The Japanese *yuki*, meaning "snow" or even "snowfall," and its curious phonetic similarities with the English "hockey" (possibly a corrupt form of the word?) suggest the Japanese concept *fuyuzare*, or "winter bareness." Hockey indeed encapsulates said mood. In addition, the lexical relation of

Yes, the palette of the hockey haiku writer is one of subdued colors and resistant hues, the only flare coming in the form of gaudy logos and jerseys (a flourish rarely overlooked by our masters). And, as William Morris famously remarked, "You can't have art without resistance in the materials." Our hockey haiku masters most assuredly have material resistance: steel, thick Plexiglas, helmets, pads, frozen pucks, and the sobering reality of ice. And this is why we must chuckle at those enlightened poet/critics of the 1980s who thought that they had stumbled onto something substantive and groundbreaking with all their talk of "whiteness" and "absences." All the while it was going on under their noses in the form of hockey haiku, which they treated in the same way William Carlos Williams treated the sonnet. They[13] seemed completely unaware of it! We are surrounded by hockey haiku, and not in that new-age Zeitgeist of trendy criticisms and passing fads. We are cookies, ourselves, contained in the jar of the hockey haiku paradigm: pucks—so to speak—in an infinite net.

---

the Japanese hokku to the English *"hockey"* indeed implies a cognate, thereby supporting the Biszt-Glesping hypothesis of the form's general exodus east over the Pacific.

[13] The Winnipeg School and their cattywampus methodologies. We do not wish them ill will but pray that at least one of them will have one-tenth the talent of a Williams (let alone of a Hull or a Dionne).

Ostensibly, the hockey haiku needs no introduction. So why yet another hockey haiku anthology, our genteel reader may ask. The reason is this: we offer here a look into the lives[14] and work of three of the most esteemed hockey haiku masters: Pat Scluney, Søren Bash-Øferdehedde, and Pyotr Fivolovic. Without a doubt, no anthology—no conversation—of hockey haiku would be complete without all three. In focusing solely on these masters, however, our goal is to distill each artist's particular gifts within this formidable art. Here, then, is a brief introduction to this anthology's storied heroes.

Pat Scluney (1893–1978)

The consummate traditionalist, Scluney led his high school hockey team to an unprecedented three province titles. We know that he shaved and collected ice from his skate blades between shifts. He then boiled the ice in a Bunsen Burner stolen from his high school chemistry class, consequently hydrating himself far after the advent of squirt bottles.[15] Born in Vancouver, British Co-

---

[14] Fivolovic's oft-quoted dictum: "You want to know my life—then read my poems; you want to know my poems—then look behind my goalie mask."
[15] Vide *Pat Scluney, A Man*, by Joe Hosey, for a biography as well researched and necessary as Peter Brown's *Augustine*.

lumbia, Scluney was the only son of a struggling postde-
cadent, prefuturist painter father and a doting mother.
He grew up in rural Vancouver, butchering goats and
boiling their heads, mending walls, milking nannies. And
it is in these stoic details that we find the deepest expression of Scluney. His Edo-style hockey haiku—like his
early life and his throwback hydration techniques—
continually harkens to simpler times. Yet times of giants.
Here, for example, we may admire his *ubi sunt* tenor:

> The empty-net goal—
> taking candy from babies:
> sad, sweet, sometimes sour.

Note how the alliterative genius in the ultimate line
strings the words together like so many pearls on a silk
thread, like the ordered goat heads on the side of a
chopping block, like the staccatoed half steps of the
goal maker on ice. Just as assuredly, though, Scluney
can also be quick to defend his art and the artifacts
within it by means of searing invectives. Observe here
his deft handling of an oft-ridiculed hockey apparatus:

> Zamboni bumper:
> Don't laugh—It crushed the leg of
> the Little Leaguer.

Scluney takes us behind the scenes, into the locker room, even into the inner workings of an ice rink, an arena. We feel what the players and rink managers themselves feel. Ever wonder what it's like to skate in circles moments before the game, the rush of adrenaline, and the counternecessity to suppress any sign of nerves? Scluney affords us a window into that world:

> There's something about
> swatting your goalie's shin pads
> postwarm-ups—Luck thuds.

To be sure, Scluney's art is recalcitrant, bold in its efficiency. He doesn't trade punches but instead drives to the net with brutal precision. We know from the meticulous locker room notes of Scluney's contemporary—historian/sportswriter Leonard Brassplutz—that Scluney's skates and underwear were both intentionally three sizes smaller in order to restrain both his speed and his libidinous nether regions in an attempt to channel all power to his hands. Eccentric? Yes, of course. (Saint Teresa of Ávila, for instance, ate her meals in the bowl of a human skull.) But Scluney was also a seeker of the most direct path to enlightenment and to the "goal" of that enlightenment.

Sadly, Scluney was cut down in his prime. Having

secured the new head coach position for the Kalamazoo K Wings, Scluney departed for a brief vacation in Italy on June 25th, 1978. He would not return to Michigan. Neither would he see his fabled, rural Vancouver, nor the goat heads again. He collapsed from anaphylactic shock, finally uttering the now infamous words: "I'm going to die, in Italy, from sunflower seeds, manufactured in Romania!" Scluney's life was one of restrictions, be it of his artistic expression, his rigorous ethics, or his nether regions. Within those self-imposed limitations, though, he managed to find an unmistakable aesthetic (and ascetic) philosophy of the game—and of life.

Søren Bash-Øferdehedde (1941–)

If the poetry of Scluney gains its importance from its cold and dogged restraint, its ghostly regular rhythms, then the poetry of Søren Bash-Øferdehedde could not be more different in its Pindaric ebullience. We might say that the notion of Pindaric hockey haiku could never have become a household concept without the pioneering work of Bash-Øferdehedde.[16] Raised as

---

[16] Note a few recent MLA conference panel titles: "Bash-Øferdehedde: Bash Over the Head, or Genius?"; "Bash-Øferdehedde and Moby-Dick: White Space as Death Incarnate"; "What Bash-Øferdehedde Can Teach Creative Writing Students Today."

the illegitimate son of Gordy Howe, only to find out at the age of eighteen that his father's name was actually Gordy Howl (a nickname given him by his boon companions), Bash-Øferdehedde—not unlike the great German poet Rilke[17]—found himself traumatized and unable at first to deal with his misguided familial history. Keeping the name of his then Swedish mother, Töve Bash—who later immigrated to Denmark in a dinghy—the young and submissive Søren befriended a Danish danish maker by the name of Øferdehedde. This pleasant if somewhat bow-legged patissier raised Søren and taught him the craft of danish making while rectifying within the lad the passion he once held for the game of hockey and, more importantly, those who played it. Indeed, Bash-Øferdehedde celebrates the athlete. Here he is at work on one of the true legends of the game still active:

Biscuit on his stick
predates a goal by seconds—
spittle on Hull's lip.[18]

---

[17] Rilke's mother, wishing she had given birth to a daughter, made young Rainer Maria wear a dress.

[18] "Biscuit" is slang for the puck. Also of note, in the Ghiberti version (one of three extant copies now housed in Milan's Archivio della Poesia Giapponese del Hockey su Ghiaccio), "twig" replaces "stick" as the favored variant.

In his distinctively middle-class lexicon—one full of local flavor, locker room jargon, and trash talking—Bash-Øferdehedde belies the fact that English was his third language (Swedish his first, Danish his second) and that hockey was his second sport (luge his first). In tandem with the bombastic, nearly Wagnerian impulse of his work, there exists a lightness of touch. A lesser hockey haiku artist, it should be noted, might concentrate, say, on the hands of Brett Hull raised into the air postgoal goalpost style, or energetically patting his teammates on the back: all the usual images we have read in the reams of mediocre hockey haiku that threaten this great art's supremacy. Rather, Bash-Øferdehedde chooses here to concentrate on the microcosm of spittle on the player's lip. Blake hardly said it better: "Hold Infinity in the Palm of your hand / And Eternity in an Hour." Careful readers will also notice the influence Bash-Øferdehedde's first sport has had on his art, the inimitable alacrity of his lines, the tautness, the lugelike centrifugality of his choices. Here, he casts his keen eye on the young New Jersey Devils forward:

> Pimpled recklessness:
> a winger with bad acne—
> it's Langenbrunner.

We experience Bash-Øferdehedde's restraint and then the accompanying drive exploding into *jouissance*. There is almost the ghost of an exclamation point after Langenbrunner's name, the poet able to embed his excitement into the winger's cheeks like so many blackheads, even as Bash-Øferdehedde eschews certain capitalizations of nouns to which he is entitled. For this is not a poet of entitlement. Here, note how he needs only his sharp wit and a gorgeously monikered goalie to convince us we are in the presence of a master:

> This next line rocks you:
> Nikolai Khabibulin.
> That last line rocked you.

There is the hint of an aesthetic so reflexive, so aware of itself both as a conduit of the past and as a contemporary mode of expression, that it borders on what authorities call the "metahockey haiku": hockey haiku that takes as its subject hockey haiku itself. Though some critics[19] have referred to his approach as

[19] How the Winnipeg School call themselves a school, we have no clue. We admit that sometimes we wish a plague of Adirondack black flies upon them and their ilk.

"the new pornography," Bash-Øferdehedde cannot be contained in such a limited and limiting pseudoeroticism.[20] He serves no master in the contemporary world but harkens back to classical Greek models, injecting into them the fervor, the p and v of a wildly contemporary lexicon. What was old is made irreversibly new in the hands of Bash-Øferdehedde.

Pyotr Fivolovic (1962–)

No discussion of metahockey haiku could be complete without the unrivaled genius of the form, Pyotr Fivolovic. Son of a clay-faced, immigrant Uzbek owner of an athletic-tape factory in Minsk, Fivolovic stakes his claim as the greatest of the metahockey haiku masters, and all at the age of forty-two.[21] Delicately and dangerously poised on the edge between the literary and the most emphatically nonliterary, between

---

[20] Okay, so we *do* hold great antipathy for the Winnipeg School. Equating a legend such as Bash-Øferdehedde with such puerile phrases as "hockey haiku barbarian" and "neofauvist"—as the Winnipeg School has done repeatedly—is nothing short of sacrilege in the name of pointless careerism. Had they any sense of true scholarship, they would have spent their time more wisely digesting Walter Rossi's monolithic *Bash-Øferdehedde: Prometheus on Ice*. But it's a big book with hardly any pictures, and that would have frightened them.

[21] Succinct and well-balanced biographical matter on Fivolovic can be found in volume two of Isa Frescott's fascinating *Blue Line, Red Line, Blue Line: Anatomy of the Hockey Haiku*.

the ink-stained fingertips of his life as an unrelenting reader and the bloodstained blades of his unerring skates, Fivolovic's art earned him with frightening speed his reputation as "most theorized" of the hockey haiku masters. His cryptic verse—relying heavily on literary precedent (clearly, he was enamored with the High Modernist mode)—is the equivalent of a *Lolita* written by Federov instead of Nabokov. He combines the artful distance of a Peace Studies think-tank consultant with the glove-befouling, sweat-drenched hands of a '70s Flyers goon. Here he is, as ever, at the top of his game, ushering into seemingly artless lines a commentary on the length of the lines themselves:

> Haiku hockey: One
> mid-ice man. At either end
> two shorter goalies.[22]

Or, in his irascible fancy, the co-opting of an Auden line to fit his purpose:

---

[22] U.S. Olympic Hockey coach Herb Brooks is said to have chanted this poem mantralike before his team took the ice against the Russians in the 1980 games. Scotty Bowman, former head coach of the Detroit Red Wings, claimed that this single poem "forced the game of hockey to reinvent itself."

> About suffering,
> they were never wrong: old guys
> stuck in the minors.[23]

In many ways, Fivolovic is, as Scluney was, a traditionalist. The difference lies in what they adhere to as tradition: Fivolovic so often looking past the game, past the haiku, into the inner mechanics of writing the verse form itself. Fivolovic asks the questions we are reluctant to ask:

> Conflict—How can I
> pledge my allegiance to two
> national anthems?

Where we admire Scluney's fluidity, we cannot help but praise what we will attempt to coin Fivolovic's "event-ness." With Fivolovic, we know that the aesthetic realm is not merely beautiful, but true and good. Fivolovic's final lines constantly remind us of arriving at a Sukiya-style Japanese tearoom. Ceremoniously, it

---

[23] In an interview with *Sports Illustrated* (December 1993), Fivolovic said he was working on a series of "narrative hockey haiku fragments" that envisioned Auden himself returning to the world as "a highly gifted winger for the Rangers, nimble in the crease but also formidable in the corners, a sort of antiromantic Tomas Sandstrom with a penchant for the burlesque."

seems as if a reader takes off his shoes in the first line, enters the austere home of the poem in line two, and finally, at an indirect angle from the entrance of the dwelling, we sidestep into the final line, ready for warm refreshment. No doubt those interested in hockey haiku theory will enjoy meditating on Fivolovic's verse enigmas. A glance at university dissertation titles in Literature and Language Departments from recent years will support his rampant ascendancy.[24]

The hockey haiku, like any hockey great, does not esteem itself, does not simply keep records of wrongs. Even in its subtle criticisms of impressive forces such as, say, Eddie Belfour, Ron Tugnutt, or Marty Turco (goalies whose rapierlike glove hands at times approach poetry), the form honors its heroes by viewing their shortcomings as heroic flaws. In essence, mere players are revealed as both mythic warriors and as ut-

---

[24] Yale as well as Duke and Northwestern have already begun interdisciplinary programs in both Metahockey Haiku and Ecohockey Haiku, though the majority of Ph.D.s in the field still graduate from West Coast schools. Of interest is also the burgeoning Postfeminist Hockey Haiku—known equally as "Hockey Gynku" or "Hockshee Haiku"—work done mainly by Tami Granato and her post-Olympiad team. The editors may only hope their research necessitates yet another hockey haiku anthology in the very near future to showcase the work of heretofore unknown women masters.

terly human. (Or, in the case of a Gretzky, at least *half*-human.) As homage to the enduring spirit of the hockey haiku itself, and in an attempt to capture the selflessness of these three masters, we have not assigned the names of the honorable trinity (Scluney, Bash-Øferdehedde, and Fivolovic) to individual poems. Apart from a desire to eschew the romanticizing of the hockey haiku, our reasons are mainly twofold: first, we are aware that even the most dedicated amateurs of hockey haiku will be able to decipher the voice emanating from each poem or will already know to whom honor belongs; secondly—and more importantly—we hope the form itself will raise the reader above such sordid realms of celebrity.

—Fleet Center, Section 12,
  Row 8, Seats 6 and 7
  Boston, MA
  2005

The winters of my childhood were long, long seasons. We lived in three places—the school, the church and the skating rink—but our real life was on the skating rink.

—Roch Carrier (from the verso of the Canadian five-dollar bill)

The Nature of the Game:

Random Cudgelings,

Dekeings, and Other Customs

1

If I had a dime

for each of their broken bones,

I'd invest in dimes.

Black fly on the pond

suddenly a black comet.

Thank you, Jumbo-Tron!

Hockey banning fights?

Who came up with this winner?

Let's cudgel his brains.

What's a two-line pass?

The referee looks tired, old.

Duh. The puck. Two lines.

Vote Wayne Gretzky for

President! In Canada

for Prime Minister!

O Canada. O,

water freezes. Centigrade.

O, it's hockey time.

I deke you, deke you.

In the crease, I deke you, you

who look sorrowful.

Though I shall deke back.

And the deked shall inherit

all this open ice.

It is not easy

to deke on the ice, unless

you are a deker.

The ref calls icing.

Everyone is dumbfounded.

There's ice everywhere.

Poor Canucks. Rich Yanks.

Expensive hockey tickets

go south. Winter geese.

Stiff cross-check—you fall

face down—Narcissus on ice.

Bloody reflection.

There's something about

swatting your goalie's shin pads

postwarm-ups—Luck thuds.

Conflict—How can I

pledge my allegiance to two

national anthems?

Five-minute major.

They score. The box remains full.

Unnecessary.

Illegal high stick?

Think again. It's in the net.

Legal high sticking.

Don't let the pink ice

fool you. This goon's lagoon ain't

for Barbies. That's blood.

There's no such thing as

wind chill to Canadians,

true fans of the game.

Shorthanded goals hurt

so good. So handy, when down:

these outnumbered ones.

We ate ice! That's what

we did before squirt bottles!

Sweat-drenched skate-shaved ice!

We thought these front row

seats were going to be great.

A hard Zen lesson.

What does my girlfriend

think when I bang the glass

oh so violently?

The old leper joke:

face-off in the corner. Win

the puck and save face.

We didn't make the

play-offs. Indeed, April is

the cruelest month.

Fans are good and bad.

For instance, it's bad to fan

the open slap shot.

Why such dreams, such hope

when they pull the goalie at

the end? They still lose.

The empty-net goal—

taking candy from babies:

sad, sweet, sometimes sour.

Berserk hockey dads

have different agendas.

Coach has a shiner.

1970s

vans never had it this good:

air-brushed goalie masks.

Another hat trick:

It's all business in the front,

party in the back.

Coast to coast, butter

on toast. But the breakaway

is eaten with jam.

What is the sound of

one stick slapping? The red light

shines; people clapping.

I cut my teeth on

roller hockey, but I broke

my teeth on the ice.

Bored at the bar or

in the family game room?

Air hockey will do.

In curling, maybe

all that sweeping helps prepare

the ice for hockey?

Some claim curling is

Canada's national sport.

Curling. What. Ever.

Women's field hockey

and men's lacrosse both lack ice.

Men's lacrosse lacks men.

Pindaric Haiku:

From Acne to Acme

2

Eddie Belfour drinks.

Eddie Belfour drinks too much.

Eddie Belfour drinks.

Bob Gainey is gone.

One by one the Stars go out.

Hitchcock cocks his neck.

Little Modano,

top shelf for the cookie jar.

Hungry Modano.

Biscuit on his stick

predates a goal by seconds—

spittle on Hull's lip.

Detroit's new savior:

Cujo's mojo in the pipes.

Hasek can't hack it.

Terror in the crease,

sacrificing teeth for goals:

Philly's John LeClair.

Valerie Bure,

tell me, if you know: What will

stop Pavel Bure?

Mario Lemieux,

are there French doppelgängers?

Yes, they are all Claudes.

This next line rocks you:

Nikolai Khabibulin.

That last line rocked you.

Coach Dave Tippett said:

"Guerins are not born on trees."

Arnotts aren't either.

Offense or defense.

Blue line, high crease, everywhere:

Sergei Federov.

Metamorphic freak:

Blackhawk, Shark, Star, now a Leaf,

Eddie the Eagle.

What is in a name?

Ron Tugnutt or Dick Trickle?

Emasculation.

Another shutout?

Is he really second string?

You tugging my nut?

Pimpled recklessness:

a winger with bad acne—

it's Langenbrunner.

See Craig McTavish.

See Craig McTavish's hair:

helmetless, feathered.

Modano's cute face:

a figure skating partner?

Arnott checks your dream.

Brett Hull thinks he can

skate on dry ice. He does: with

his Red Wings rising.

Hasek and Hatcher?

What is up with the Hs?

Happy Hull has help.

O Donald Brasheer,

Flying face first into glass:

Love yourself, your face.

Old pint-sized Blackhawk,

Liquored up, dressed up: off ice

Fleury flaps his lips.

During the game, it's

Jagr: Master. Afterwards,

it's Jägermeister.

Modano's so cute

I want to throw roses on

the ice. But I don't.

I swear! Foiled again.

H-E-double hockey sticks.

Satan's in the crease.

The penalty box

ultimate. Satan on ice.

Dante would be proud.

Aging Rangers brat—

Concussion-laden Canuck—

Lindros out again.

King with concussions

became headstrong new head coach—

Alas, Granato.

Bad midlife mullet.

Chewing gum won't restore youth.

Barry Melrose: Why?

Can't muss it up, Mess-

ier's hair, and all those hats

doffed to the bald ice.

Lang, turn the light low

and play her some Barry White.

Unmask her goalie.

Hockey without fights.

Belfour without a stiff drink.

Screw your Lady Byng!

Eddie Belfour swills,

pees Boston Bruins yellow

in a holding cell.

Gretzky, hockey stick

preslap shot: a goalie's grim

reaper, scythe held high.

Gordy Howe's weapon?

A wooden stick sweet on ice:

cherry pop-sickle.

Bad Dallas cliché:

"Falling Stars." Make a wish for

burned-out Modano.

Even with the blue

mask blocking, Belfour's eyes are

Arctic iceberg blue.

It's Jason Priestley!

It's Celebrity Hockey!

No, Jason Priestley!

Wayne Gretzky's 3-D

Hockey doesn't quite capture

His 4-D hockey.

Hockey mask thriller:

Are you Jason Voorhees or

Mike Ricci? Scary.

His doughy face jars,

but still the Avalanche fall

for him: Foote fetish.

Walter and Phyllis

Gretzky, I wanted to say:

thanks for Wayne Gretzky.

Intermission & Stoppage:

(Including Guesswork Regarding

Arena Urinals)

3

Hotdogs clog the throat.

Beer's plastic chalice held high:

It's intermission.

Molsen Ice, Bud Light.

The long, faithless pilgrimage

to the urinal.

Zamboni bumper:

Don't laugh—It crushed the leg of

the Little Leaguer.

We score, and then this

music: Duh dum duh dum duh

dum duh duuuh dum. HEY!

This beer is good, ay?

Golden colour, nice flavour:

Canadiens can't spell.

Come on feel the noise.

Bored fans wait for the face-off.

Song interrupted.

Did you sneak in a

can of beer or are you just

happy to see me?

Was Vanilla Ice

a loser? Yes, but . . . stoppage

airs "Ice, Ice, Baby"

Dumb intermission

games, while the team four-down gets

a vulgar earful.

The Standings,

Mascot Mockery and Veneration

4

Ubi sunt Canucks.

Winnipeg went far away.

A coyote yips.

Bottom of the league,

the Thrashers thrash in the muck.

Their logo is weak.

What kind of mascot

is a freaking maple leaf?

Scratchy, doomed to fall.

I'm a Maple Leaf!

Fear my blue fall, my scratchy

edge! I could blind you.

Florida Panthers:

O the briefest dynasty.

Those rats were silly.

Los Angeles Kings

rule nothing but the basement.

Los Angeles Queens.

Los Angeles Kings

are in the cellar again,

should invest in wine.

Question, Toronto:

I understand the leaf, but

why blue? Cold up there?

Who is farthest South?

As far as the standings go,

Florida Panthers.

I don't know if it's

a pleasing idea to have

the Ducks win the cup.

Surreal sharks circling

above the ice. Only in

Califor-nye-a.

Blues and Blue Jackets.

Both lackluster teams this year.

Why do I feel sad?

What's so Wild about
Minnesota? Ten thousand
lakes fill up with tears.

Tampa Bay Lightning,
Carolina Hurricanes.
Summer conditions?

It was the best ice

when the Stars won. When they lost,

it was the worst ice.

Ice-cold ice. Hotdog.

Hockey game in June, Phoenix

rising from the smog.

Penguin (Canada)

rejection slip. Did they want

more Penguins or Leafs?

Cowboy poetry

can't round up the majesty:

Lubbock Cotton Kings.

Buffalo Sabres

have a buffalo mascot,

no sword. This is Zen.

Lowercase won't do.

THE WASHINGTON CAPITALS

ARE MONUMENTAL.

Buoyant Mighty Ducks

are worthy adversaries

of the lithe Penguins.

Metahockey Haiku:

Are You Marty Turco?

5

Haiku hockey. One

mid-ice man. At either end

two shorter goalies.

In hockey, we say,

"the ice," which is to say, ice

transcends space-time stuff.

Is the puck awkward

to you or is it just me?

Are you Marty Turco?

A hockey stick is

the *L* plucked from the word "pluck."

What's left should be struck.

O hockey haiku:

He who made the lamb made thee,

our hockey haiku.

Heretofore unseen:

Anabaptist Pacifists

in hockey haiku.

She says, "Bull Hockey!"

Euphemisms are just not

what they used to be.

Speaking Japanese,

we would know that *hokku* means

wet rice, and hockey.

Three lines in haiku

hockey. The stick my brute pen.

I jones for winter.

Two skates diverged in

a crowded crease, and that has

made all the difference.

Huffy Henry hid

the puck. Uncheckable, he

was uncheckable.

I heard a fly buzz.

Or that Philly Flyer Burke

just concussed my head.

About suffering

they were never wrong: old guys

stuck in the minors.

She sang beyond the

genius of the ice. She sang

both national anthems.

Much depends upon

a Red Wing glazed with Duck blood

after fisticuffs.

I knew a woman.

When Mike Modano sighed, she

would sigh back at him.

Men at forty learn

to close softly the lockers

they won't come back to.

All the new thinking

is about hockey haiku.

Like the old thinking.

Hockey haiku, then

volleyball villanelle. Next?

Limerick de luge.

Eddie Belfour drinks.

Virgil Suarez writes too much.

Eddie Belfour drinks.

Let us go then, you

and I, as the home team is

just stinking it up.

Lydwina, Patron

Saint of Skaters, do you pray

for Mike Modano?

5-7-5? Check

Bludgeoned pencil, bleeding eyes?

Hockey haiku? Check.

The Hockey Haiku:

This panel seeks to define

the hockey haiku.

O Richard Howard,

be my verse coach, my sensei,

my own Kurt Russell.

Stick and glove hover

at the goalie's sides. He is

vertical haiku.

My home page is set:

Hockeyology.com

I will hack your face!

Lady Byng is kind

of cruel. Cruel and kind,

she asks for martyrs.

I was of two minds:

The prechecked, unbloodied one,

and the foul other.

The Lockout and Season's Return:

Heroic Homeric Hockey Haiku,

Including Invocation of the Muses

6

X-box irony.

My hockey game just froze up.

Like the NHL!

Comedy of Errors.

Much Ado About Nothing.

No hockey, Shakespeare.

You sat and watched me

as I sat and pined for games

meager as a puck.

Under the hardwood

of basketball arenas,

ice quietly waits.

Ugliest hat trick

is the reason no season:

the salary cap.

Dude, where's my hockey?

Ashton Kutcher stars in this

tragic comedy.

No pen or skate will

scribble any haiku or

hockey this season.

Lockout or strike? What's

the difference to a fan

jonesing for goons.

Who owns my wordplay?

The hockey haiku lockout.

Writer's block of ice.

Halfway through last year,

hockeyless, I lost it. Hell,

the season on ice.

Rage, sing Goddess, of

Peleus' son, Achilles,

or hockey season.

Speak, Muse, of the Wild,

Islander, Ranger, returned

to home ice. Face-off!